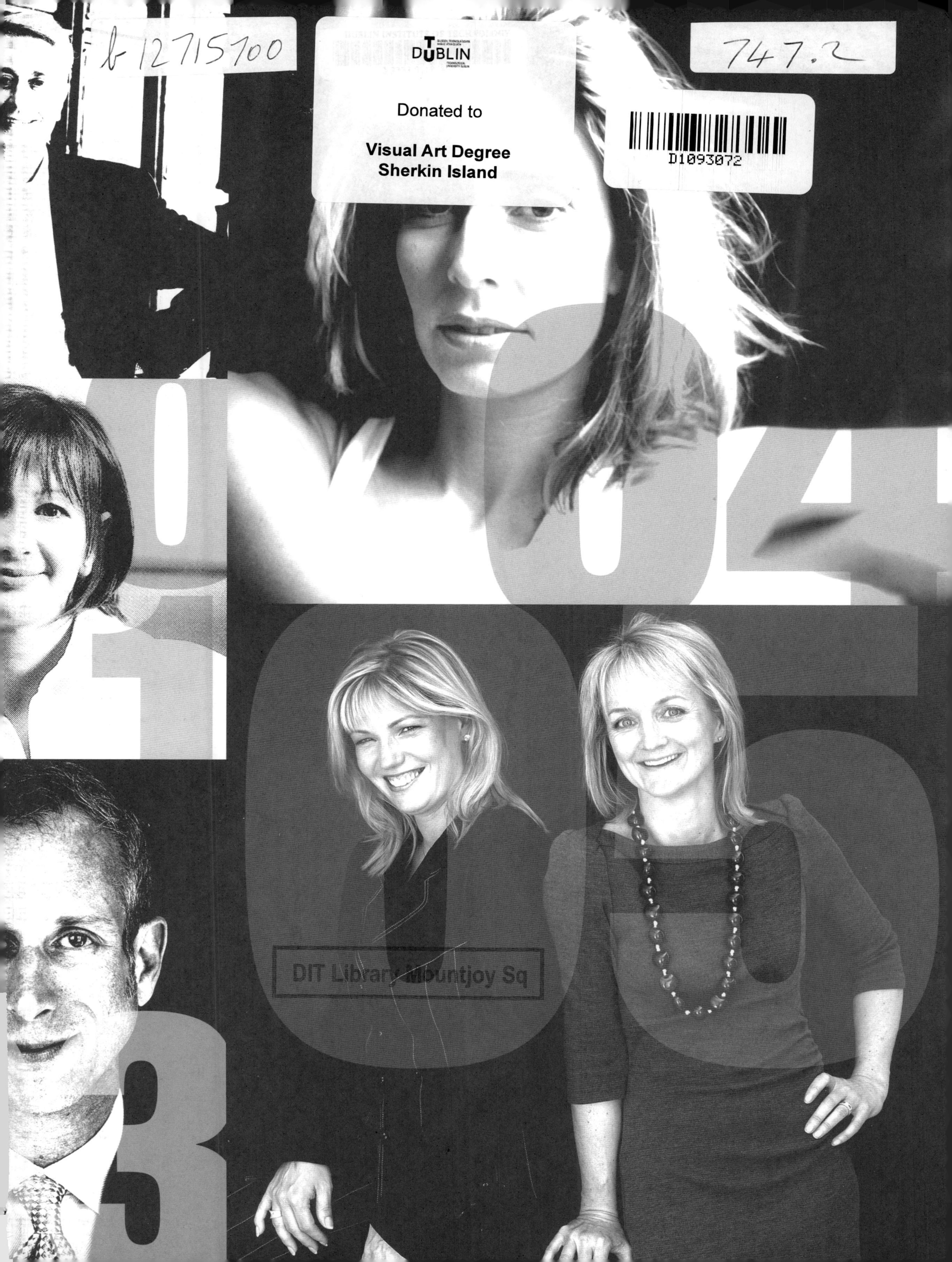

Interior Design Review Volume 10

Martin Waller
Daisy Bridgewater

ANDREW MARTIN
INTERNATIONAL

ANDREW MARTIN

Editor: Martin Waller
Text: Daisy Bridgewater
Project Executive: Annika Bowman
Product Design: Graphicom Design

First Published in 2006 by Andrew Martin International

ISBN 0-9530045-8-9

Reproduction by Lamplight Group.
Printed in Singapore by Craft Print International Ltd.

Acknowledgements
The author and publisher wish to thank all the owners and
designers of the projects featured in this book.

They also thank the following photographers:
Tim Evan Cook, Hugo Burnand, Iain Kemp, Christian
Rochat, John Peden, Ken Hayden, Cees Roelofs, Bieke
Claessens, Ronny Vanthienen, Studio d'Arte, Matthu
Placek, Abbey Drucker, Reto Guntli, Nacasa & Partners
Inc, Takeshi Nakasa, Toshio Nagao, Juan Rodriguez,
Martin Garcia Perez, Juan Manuel Miranda Santana,
Dook, Silvio Rech, Lesley Carstens, Andy Payne, Mike
Myers, Ted Yarwood, Shelagh Howard, Luke White, James
Balston, Christopher Cornwell, Steve Freihon, Lisa
Kereszi, Michael Moran, Dominic Albo, Gerald Steiner,
Richard Waite, Chris Tubbs, Ales Jungmann, James
Morris, Giorgio Baroni, Sargent photography, Michael
Crockett, Chris Tubbs, Joao Frazao, James Mortimer,
Tessa Kennedy, Ella Pellegrini, John Martin, Carolin
Knabbe, Werner Prokschi Architekturphotographie,
Warren Smith Photography, ST James Group Ltd, William
Cummings, Helen Tschudi, Stefan Jannides, Ulso Tsang,
Steve Mok, Richard Seaton, Bob Marchant, Klaus Jordan,
Virginia Lung, Doc Ross, Yoshio Shiratori, Mauro Pini,
Gavin Kingcome, Nikos Papadopoulos, George Lizardos,
Harry Hristopoulos, Vangelis Paterakis, Kostas
Mitropoulos, Margareth De Lange, James Hudson, Ddiarte:
Diamantino Jesus, Ze Diogo, Alma Mollemans, Benno
Thoma, Brian Benson, John Gott, Warren Smith, Andreas
von Einsiedel, Hugo Burnand, David Garcia, Craig Dugan,
Jim Hedrich, Jeffrey Millis, David Schilling, Bruce Van
Inwegen, Steve Becker, Nacasa and Partners, Second
Wind, Eduardo Pozella, Alain Brugier, Francisco Almeida
Dias, Tim Beddow, Mark Luscombe-Whyte, Patrick
Tyberghein, Accor, Sofitel, Club Med, Marc Hertrich,
Charlotte Wood, Henri Bourne, Michael Crockett, Ricky
Zehavi, Joseph Sy, Cindy Anderson, Annette Fischer,
Kawasumi Architectural Photograph Office, Michael
Scates, Bruce Hemming, Amanda Jackson, Joao Bessone,
Nuno Teixeira, David Marlow Photography, Brantley
Photography, Shelagh Howard, Gordon Beall, Thibault
Jeanson, Grey Crawford and Alan Shortall.

The carousel of fashion never stops turning. It always astonishes me how we can all date the age of houses to within 10 years, even if they were built 300 years ago. Furniture, glass, silverware can be dated with ferocious exactitude. When we think how fast the years slip by in our own lives, it is a source of wonder to reflect on the endless ingenuity of designers. The need to reinvent and repackage is nothing new. The same is true of interiors in any decade of the 20th Century. We know exactly how Edwardian London looked or deco New York or 50's Paris. Style may stand the test of time but time stands still for no style.

With the tyranny of minimalism firmly behind us, rather like Cavalier Restoration poets, designers are discovering the forbidden fruit of fabric. Throughout history, fabric has defined peoples and cultures as much as art or architecture. Scottish tartan, French brocade, West African Kuba, English flannel, American denim are all short hand for national stereotypes.

Weaving, dying, finishing are one of civilisation's miracles that is utterly taken for granted. For centuries, cloth was one of the world's most precious commodities. It was an emblem of power and wealth. In Imperial Rome, wearing purple without the Emperor's permission was punishable by death. During the Renaissance, tapestries were much more valuable than the masterpiece of painting we now so revere. Mytens got £66 for his famous portrait of Charles I. The King's tailor got £266 for the suit the King is wearing in the picture. Silk was the great state secret of ancient China and valued by its weight in gold. Until comparatively recently, fabric was a currency more trusted than gold or goats in the Congo region.

Throughout history, textiles have driven international trade. The medieval wool merchants built England's great churches. By the end of the 17th Century, textiles represented half of England's exports. By the 19th Century the Industrial Revolution was powered by weaving and the dark satanic mills of Lancashire were the rock on which England's economic dominance was forged.

So it's really no great surprise to see the resurgence of fabric in the home. Fabric is welded into our historic psyche. We rediscover it with the joy with which we might revisit a favourite childhood book. And today more than ever we can revel in the startling variety of textures and colours brought forth from every corner of the globe. It's a pleasure to see it back on the agenda of the world's designers.

Martin Waller

Gail Taylor & Karen Howes

**Designers : Gail Taylor & Karen Howes.
Company: Taylor Howes Designs, London.
Projects: International design agency
providing a comprehensive service for private
clients, property developers and hoteliers.
Recent commissions include a Thames
penthouse, a new build private house outside
Dublin and the refurbishment of an 18,000
square foot Belgravia house.**

Moon worshipping best friends who are too exhausted to dream, worn out by the burden of perfectionism and an intense disliking for flocked wallpaper. Karen would love a huge pink diamond and ownership of Canary Wharf. Gail legs like Elle Mcpherson, a better command of French and a sportier disposition

True Anglophiles, they would have no other city but London as their base and rather wished they had designed the London Eye

Where Karen would be Prime Minister, Gail would be Kate Moss but both would play backing piano for Sting any day

11

Federica Palacios

Designer: Federica Palacios.
Company: Federica Palacios Design, Geneva.
Projects: Domestic projects and boutique hotels around Europe, including chalets in Zermatt and the spa of the Grand Hotel Park in Gstaad.

Heat seeking, com
loving designer w
taller and be able

puter hating, children
uld love to grow 5cm
o read people's minds

She wishes that she had designed the Waterfall House by Frank Lloyd Wright and

would like to be a Formula One racer for the day

or the drummer for Police

She dreams of having a chauffeur and thinks

the world would be a better place without fluorescent colours

Richard Adams

Designer: Richard Adams.
Company: Richard Adams Interiors, London.
Projects: Small, exclusive high end residential projects in the UK, Middle East and Europe.

Highly civilised, immaculately dressed dreamer who finds it difficult to ask for money. Was once taken hostage by Chechen rebels

Would like to captain a luxury liner and throw a party at the Metropolitan Museum. Takes comfort in cats and bespoke tailoring. Reveres the diamond cufflink, loathes Battersea Power Station. Harbours a desire to play the piano in the orchestra at the Royal Opera. Could not live without ice

Jan des Bouvrie

**Designer: Jan des Bouvrie.
Company: Ontwerpstudio Jan des Bouvrie,
Naarden, Holland. Projects: Established, high
end interior designer and architect, working on
everything from international hotels and
private houses to furniture and product design.**

Cigar-toting family man who credits himself with having changed the face of the Dutch interior. Struggles with the fact that he isn't immediately understood. Would like to communicate with horses. Dyslectic. Creative

Dreams of owning an Art Deco building in Miami and of falling asleep on his wife

Jaak Langenberg & Brigitte Vanzonhoven

Designers: Jaak Langenberg
& Brigitte Vanzonhoven.
Company: Montagna Lunga, Limburg, Belgium.
Projects: Private houses and hotels.

Happy, passionate and imaginative designers who liken the completion of projects to giving birth and want to be seen as good-hearted artists. Brigitte admits to being insecure and wishing she was 10cm taller. Jaak is a perfectionist with a large appetite and a disdain for Nouvelle Cuisine

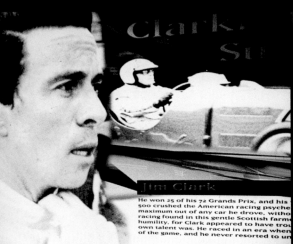

Jim Clark

He won 25 of his 72 Grands Prix, and his
500 crushed the American racing psyche
maximum out of any car he drove, witho
racing found in this gentle Scottish farme
humility, for Clark appeared to have trou
own talent was. He raced in an era when
of the game, and he never resorted to un

Brigitte wishes she had designed Tarzan's tree house and longs for a private tour of Madonna's kitchen. Jaak is waiting for an invitation to drum for Kylie Minogue. Both genuinely believe they can talk to their dog, Winston

Cara Zolot & Elizabeth Kohn

Designers: Cara Zolot & Elizabeth Kohn.
Company: ZK Interiors, New York.
Projects: Hip interior design and project management team, providing everything from initial planning to lighting, furniture and art selection. Recent projects include Upper Eastside apartments and a Miami Beach Waterfront property.

Canine-friendly New Yorkers who would like to predict the future and see Bush out of office. They long for a long and healthy life and a Christmas full of Ipod Nanos. Perfection would be a bed with a view of Malibu Beach and a secret life performing guitar and back-up vocal with Coldplay. Would love to work in London but would really rather be in Fiji or anywhere warm and tropical

Serdar Gülgün

Designer: Serdar Gülgün.
Company: Serdar Gülgün, Turkey.
Projects: Ottoman style residential and
hotel projects, working particularly with
traditional buildings and people who
are art collectors.

Multi-disciplined, highly selectiv
like to work with a view of the
of Mehmet the Conqueror and l

and deeply suspicious of power, he would
rdens of Shalimar, own Benini's portrait
his hair down in Beijing's Forbidden City

As happy in a lighthouse in the middle of the Bosphorus as resting on the bosom of Sophia Loren, he sees his potential as a whirling Sufi Dervish. Or a diplomat

Toshio Nagao

Designer: Toshio Nagao.
Company: Kenmochi Design Associates,
Tokyo, Japan. Projects: International
commercial and residential design,
including interior design, furniture
design, signage and display.

A design purist with a loathing for Neo-Classicism and mobile telephones, he would happily work from a hut in a forest for the love of his job not the money it earns him. Dreams of swimming through the air and working some place other than Japan. At pains to be more self-sacrificing, would choose a lady's thigh over a pillow and would prefer a slightly larger chest

Catherine Grenier

Designer: Catherine Grenier.
Company: Atelier de Catherine, Madrid, Spain. Projects: Offices, showrooms, restaurants, spas and hotels. Working closely with the new Madrid T4 airport and the Fast Good restaurant chain.

Vespa-riding, soufflé making, self-proclaimed psychiatrist who wishes she had darker hair and lived nearer to her family. Still not recovered from choosing her wedding dress, still not reconciled with financial restrictions and still trying to work out why her house is invaded by ants for 2 weeks every year

Wishes her neighbours would stop having barbecues and that mankind would leave the world's natural resources alone

Silvio Rech & Lesley Carstens

Designers: Silvio Rech & Lesley Carstens.
Company: Silvio Rech & Lesley Carstens Architecture and Interiors, Johannesburg, South Africa.
Projects: Bush camps, lodges and hotels celebrating African style and using traditional skills and craftsmen, plus high end residential projects and furniture design.

Innovative, footloose and fre
site under canvas - on the Se
Okavango Delta - to get the
process begins. Would live
monastery with monks serv

-thinking, they spend months on
engeti Plains or floodplains of the
eel of a place before the design
in a deconsecrated minimalist
g high percentage alcohol on tap

Daydream during accounting sessions of hungry lionesses and prowling hyena and of communicating with elephants. Long to be thinner and to wear comfortable shoes

Powell & Bonnell

**Designers: David Powell & Fenwick Bonnell.
Company: Powell & Bonnell, Toronto, Canada.
Projects: Custom interiors for an international
clientele in both residential and commercial design.
The company also produce a range of lighting,
furnishings and textiles.**

Gentlemen who feel old enough to do what they please and enjoy the freedom which that knowledge brings. Fenwick thinks his greatest achievement was to be born headfirst, while David doesn't think he has achieved it yet. Both wish they had learnt some of life's lessons sooner and would like the ability to make people perpetually happy. David thinks kittens should be worshipped, Fenwick thinks they should be used to stuff pillows. David would like to eliminate greed, Fenwick would like laughter to be the cure for cancer

the g hotel

Owner:
Gerry Barrett

Design Director:
Philip Treacy

Architect:
Colin Jennings

**Interior Design
Co-ordinator:** Aurora Aleson

Bonsai-worshipping, highly co-ordinated wannabe ballroom dancer who loathes his knees. Dreams of jumping on his magic carpet and taking his pet panda to Antarctica, of seeing icebergs from his bed and of repairing the ozone layer. Would like to escape the matrix and relocate to Cloud 9, spend a week on the Virgin Galactic and rid the world of plastic

Gerry Barrett

Pip Isherwood & Karen Batchelor

**Designers: Pip Isherwood & Karen Batchelor.
Company: Isherwood Interior Design,
Cheltenham, Gloucestershire.
Projects: Predominantly residential in
London, the South West and the Cotswolds.**

Water-loving girls' girls who long for a coastal office in Cornwall and more holidays with their friends. Pip wants new knees, self-cleaning hair and to share a bedroom with George Clooney. Karen will settle for a ban on artex ceilings and eternal praise for her karaoke rendition of Barbra Streisand's 'Enough is enough'

If heaven is a hot water bottle, a cup of tea and some scones in the comfort of the Musée Rodin in Paris,

hell is wearing shoulder pads in a Mock Tudor mansion

Sig Bergamin

Designer : Jose Antonio.
Company: Sig Bergamin Arquitetura,
Sao Paulo, Brazil. Projects: International
residential and commercial.

Impatient, well-travelled pacifist who sleeps in Technicolor and won't go anywhere without his toothbrush. Mostly to be found on a big comfortable sofa watching television or dozing in his beach house at Trancoso

Would like to spend more time maintaining his peace of mind and building up his bank balance. Longs to sneak into clients' houses and rearrange their furniture

Christina Sullivan & Susan Bednar Long

Designers: Christina Sullivan &
Susan Bednar Long.
Company: Tocar, New York.
Projects: High end residential and
commercial interiors including restaurants,
fitness centres and motor yachts.

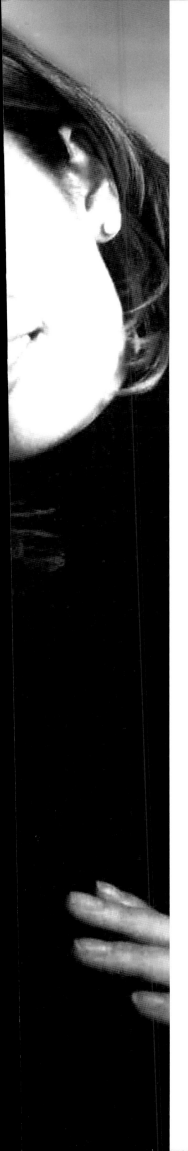

Celebrity-obsessed new mother, Susan dreams of pushing Angelina Jolie off a chair lift and looking like Cameron Diaz. She would settle for a permanent tan and a never ending supply of freshly cut flowers and would be delighted if the phrase 'you go girl' was banned from use

Christina thinks ostrich eggs should be worshipped as a new religion. Ideally she would work from a cabana in Mexico, live in a bungalow in Bora Bora and sleep in Louis XIV's bedroom at Versailles. She thinks Florence is the most romantic city on earth but would elope to Las Vegas

Francesco Saporita

Designers: Philip Pelletier & Francesco Saporita.
Company: Vie Interieur, Switzerland.
Projects: Private and commercial from shops
and restaurants to a recent refurbishment of a
Swiss castle for American clients.

Fantasy time travellers who believe in the power of love and want to give up smoking. Angelic as children, as grown-ups they would like a bit more sex, drugs and rock 'n roll. Would like to remove stress from their lives with a vacuum cleaner and cannot imagine life without washing machines

Have designs on the Statue of Liberty and with the wave of a magic wand would turn coloured pencils into religious objects and talk to birds and butterflies

Helen Green

Designer: Helen Green.
Company: Helen Green Design, London.
Projects: Exclusive private and public commissions including the Sandpiper Hotel in Barbados, the suites of the Berkeley Hotel and the interior of a 90 metre super yacht.

Frighteningly focussed, obsessed with time-keeping, plagued by bureaucracy. As a child she would torment her siblings by restyling their bedrooms. Gets most comfort in life out of cashmere and her grandmother's Regency jardinière and would like to see everything sugar-coated

She would love Anna Wintour's job but could not live without her Subzero fridge

Jestico + Whiles

Designers: Jestico + Whiles.
Company: Jestico + Whiles, London.
Projects: A team of architects and designers specialising in hotels, restaurants, apartments and cinemas. Work in progress includes the Chinese Embassy and a series of multiplex cinemas across India.

Share a collective fear of perms, addicted to hair-dryers, wish it didn't rain so much

Would like to control other people's minds, work for Mies van der Rohe and have a chill out area at work. Operate as one and would spend group bonding time at the Blue Lagoon in Iceland

Stefano Dorata

Designer: Stefano Dorata.
Company: Stefano Dorata Architetto, Rome, Italy.
Projects: Architect with private and commercial
projects in Italy and internationally.

High achieving highly focussed only child who enjoys power over other people and the sight of his own reflection. Would like to live in an igloo with views of the sea and to learn to communicate with giraffes. Could not live without his pencil

Obsessed with flying, he is currently trying to sprout wings. A self proclaimed pacifist who would like to be a fighter pilot for the day

Allison Paladino

Designer: Allison Paladino.
Company: Allison Paladino, Palm Beach.
Projects: Custom interiors from construction to furnishing in high end interiors and yachts throughout the USA.

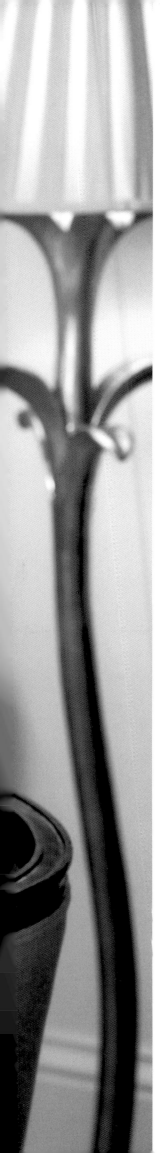

Ambitious vegetable addict, would like to own The Louvre and all its contents and be trusted by all mankind. Influenced by Alice in Wonderland and Tom Pheasant. Terrified of hang-gliding. Would rid the world of plastic covering on upholstered furniture and weapons of mass destruction

Dreams of being a easting working with sea creature moment at the Rachamanka Mai, Thailand

lirector and of
. Had a sexy
Hotel in Chiang

Luigi Esposito

Designer: Luigi Esposito.
Company: Forma Designs, London.
Projects: Residential and commercial design including shops, restaurants and a polo club.

Native Brazilian with a love of wood and a desire to be richer. Could do with a manicure and would like to be permanently slim and happy. Thinks the best gift is a 21 day detox and would happily spend a week in a Tibetan monastery. Would like to blow up the Gherkin and throw a party in the courtyard at the Victoria and Albert Museum

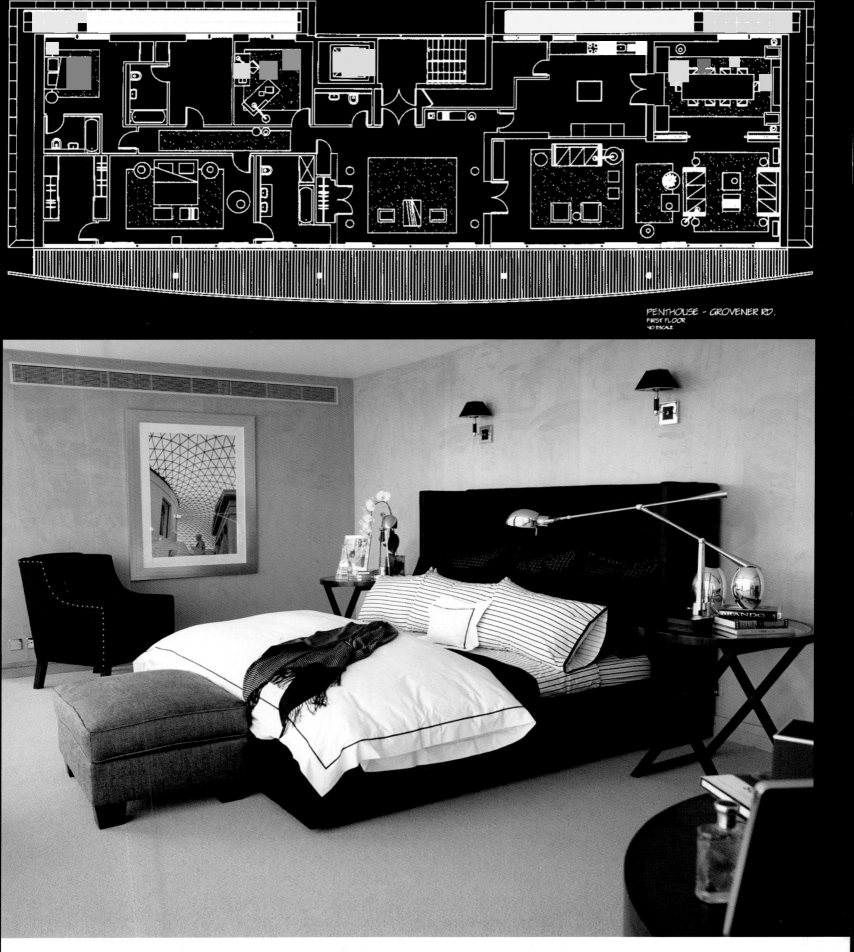

PENTHOUSE - GROVENER RD.
FIRST FLOOR
NO ESCALE

Currently house-hunting but would settle for the Vatican
and values his faith above all earthly possessions

131

Horsey, happily married pacifist w
years and spread happiness and cho
on New York and Michelangelo's sta
a fairy godmother and a chance to b
describe their work as simpl
contemplate life without silence, s

Luisa Reimao Pinto & Paula Gallego

**Designers: Luisa Reimao Pinto & Paula Gallego.
Company: K. arq-Arquitectos Associados,
Lisbon, Portugal. Projects: Houses, apartments,
offices, hotels, restaurants, commercial and
public buildings in Portugal and Spain.**

o would like to turn the clock back 10
plate around the world. Luisa has her eye
le of David, while Paula is holding out for
the best polo player in the world. Both
and exquisite and neither could
a views and their respective husbands

137

Tessa Kennedy

Successful, stylish and satisfied, would change little about her life apart from growing blonde hair and long thin legs

Designer: Tessa Kennedy.
Company: Tessa Kennedy
Design, London.
Projects: Established,
international company
with several interior
design accolades and a
number of illustrious
clients (including royals
and rock stars). Diverse
projects range from
luxury residential work
to grand hotels and
casinos.

Has designs on outer-space and would like to sing with the Rolling Stones. Sleeps in a chapel in a gothic bed with no recurring dreams, only nightmares about minimalism and managing agents

Would like a large yacht,
a party in Versailles and
a long conversation with
a whale

Tim Harris

Designer: Tim Harris.
Company: Tim Harris Interiors, Australia.
Projects: Customised luxury homes and commercial spaces. Recent projects include a modern cattle ranch and a luxury beach house.

Bold, brave and empowering, he wants to be recognised for powder rooms that make you feel special. Not good in the mornings. Would prefer to be sitting next to the Trevi fountain in Rome. Torments his siblings whenever he has the opportunity. Has collected Vogue Living and Belle magazine since he was 13. Would like to own the Holy Grail or the Sydney Opera House. Hates grunge

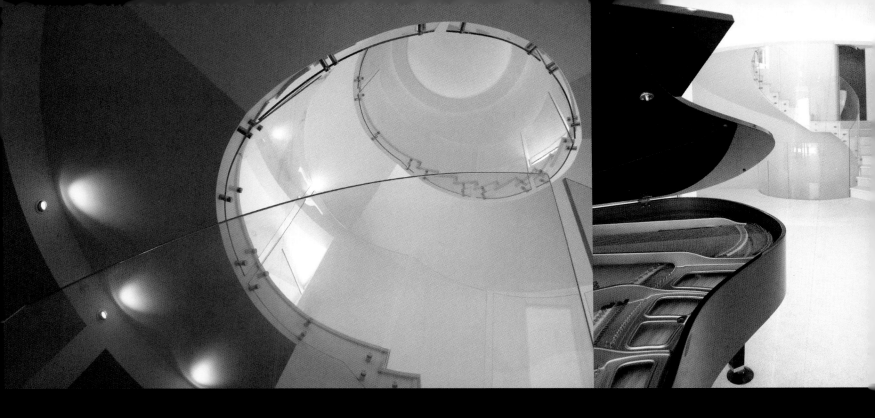

Loves his wedding band. Would elope anywhere with childcare. Thinks the best discoveries are made out back

Kiki Schröder &

**Designers: Kiki Schröder & Peter Buchberger.
Company: Buchberger Schröder, Munich, Germany.
Projects: Young urban practice working on
commercial design throughout Germany and in
Spain, France and Switzerland.**

Peter Buchberger

Workaholics with punctuality problems and a taste for red Bordeaux, they wish they had designed the Guggenheim in New York and could be opera tenors in another life

They have no dreams but wish they could read the minds of others

Would spend the summer in Alaska and the night in the Coco Chanel suite at the Ritz in Paris but would not change a thing about their workspace - they designed it themselves

Christopher Dezille

Designer: Christopher Dezille.
Company: Honky Design, London.
Projects: Design consultancy taking on commercial and private projects in central London, including some large apartments in Belgravia and houses in Kensington.

Plagued by park by litter, addic wouldn't change

ng tickets, troubled
ed to liquorice, he
thing about his life

Likes nothing more than a stretch and a deep breath. Advocate of the comfortable bed and soft pillow, though would prefer to rest his head on his wife, Sarah

Would have liked to work for Charles and Ray Eames and to ask a lemming 'Why?'

William Cummings

Designers: Bernt Heiberg & William Cummings.
Company: Heiberg Cummings Design, New York & Oslo.
Projects: Scandinavian-influenced residential and commercial projects in Europe and the USA and a collection of furniture which references the use of raw materials and simple colours in 19th Century Norwegian interiors.

Impossibly ambitious neo-Scandinavians who like to make people happy and dream of world peace, eating mashed potatoes and smashing mobile telephones to pieces with rocks

Would rather be on Mykonos or at the Charlotte Inn in Martha's Vineyard

With a bit of Botox here and there
would happily share the stage with Cher

Monica Blinco-Lynch

Designer: Monica Blinco-Lynch.
Company: Blinco Interior Design, Hamilton, Australia.
Projects: Large private residential projects including the restoration of a Portofino style house and a new build French villa-style residence.

Honest, intuitive, positive-thinking juice-freak would like to live on Lake Como in a world where thongs had never been invented

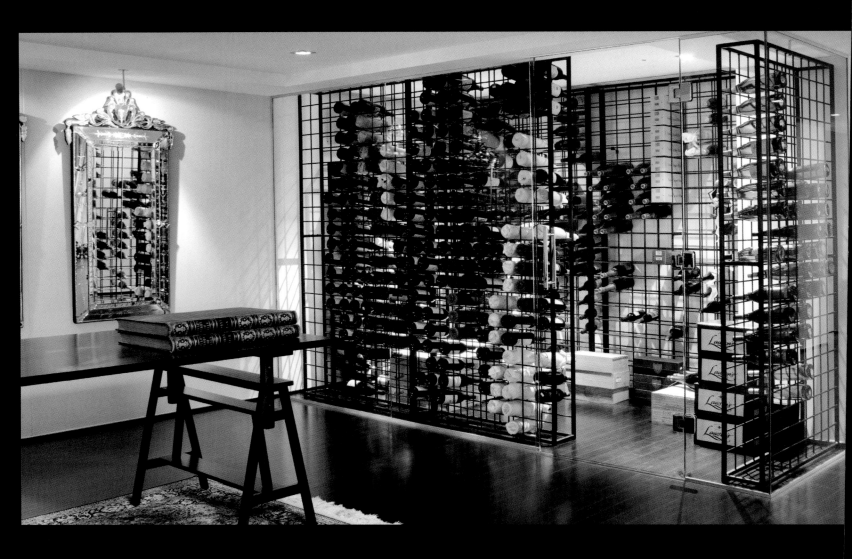

Worships her husband and thinks others should too. Their daughter is her greatest achievement so far

Would party in Sweden's Ice Hotel and seek solitude on the West Coast of Ireland and takes most comfort in silence

Joao Maria

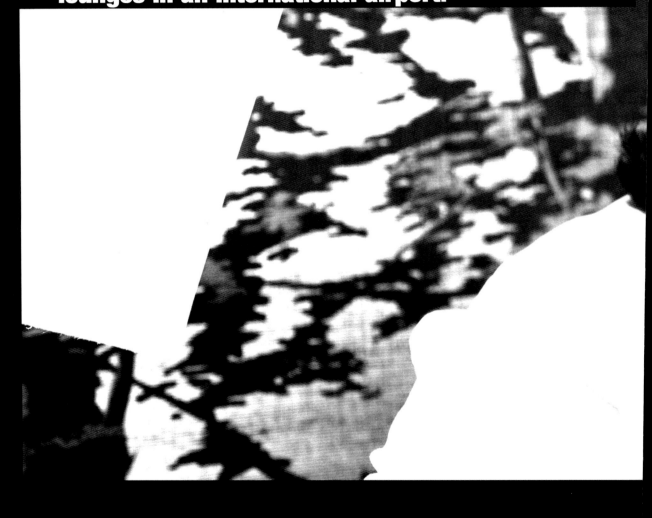

Designer: Joao Maria.
Company: Abrindo Portas, Setubal, Portugal.
Projects: Interior design company working in the private and public sectors in Portugal and internationally. Projects are worked on from architectural construction through to the finishing touches. Current projects include a luxury beach complex and the refurbishment of lounges in an international airport.

Daring, existen
genius who drea
to the world an

alist, self-proclaimed
s of showing his work
changing his haircut

He fantasises about flying and a world without George Bush. Would gladly spend the day as a city road sweeper and the night partying at the Electricity Museum in Lisbon

Would like to play sax with Woody Allen and live in the Sanderson Hotel but would not come out without his closet

Steve Leung

Designer: Steve Leung.
Company: Steve Leung Designers, Hong Kong.
Projects: Predominantly high end commercial work, from club houses and hotels to shopping malls, throughout the major developed cities in China.

Tone deaf former sportsman who finds most comfort in life in sleep. Would be a chef in his own boutique hotel in another life but for now dreams of a pair of wings and a life where the lift isn't constantly out of order

Loves romantic
Somewhere in Time a
in Yunnan the most

ovies, particularly
finds the Shangri-La
autiful spot on earth

Terence Disdale

Designer: Terence Disdale.
Company: Terence Disdale Design, Richmond, Surrey.
Projects: Yacht designer specialising in exterior and interior design of super-yachts, luxury motor and sailing yachts.

Water loving adventurer who gets his creative stimulus camping by remote Indian rivers where he once caught an 84lb mahseer. His selective short term memory loss makes him free from burdens. He often breaks the mould and works in an eclectic modern style for his yacht interiors

Virginia Lung & Law Ling Kit

Designers: Virginia Lung & Law Ling Kit.
Company: One Plus Partnership, Hong Kong.
Projects: Residential and commercial in
Hong Kong, China and Singapore.

Hard-working partners seek super model statistics and a busier social life. Virginia finds most comfort at home but wishes to be free from the burden of her family. Law just wishes we were all naturalists

Virginia would like to communicate with aliens. Both would like their minds to stay active and to spend a week alone and away from civilisation in Paris

Susie Paynter & Teassa Paynter

Designers: Susie Paynter & Teassa Paynter.
Company: Paynter Design, Christchurch, New Zealand.
Projects: Comprehensive interior design and project management for high end residential work from large scale private estates to apartments.

Vertically challenged hill walkers who loathe housework and cigarettes in equal measure. Would perform better around a well-stocked bar and think an electronic fly swat worthy of worship

They yearn to spend an hour in private nosing around Tom Ford's home and would not have minded working for Ralph Lauren

Would party in Ankor Wat, elope to New York and love to be more organised but are basically never happier than at home, as long as there is a washing machine

Takashi Sugimoto

Designer: Takashi Sugimoto.
Company: Super Potato Co,
Tokyo, Japan. Projects: Large
scale commercial, from
shopping malls to holiday
resorts and hotels.

Motorcycle rider who dr

golf handicap and seeks

ms of daintiness and a better
lace in rural Japan in autumn

Would happily spend a week walking the silk route from Turpan to Kaxgar, would elope to Shanghai and relocate his workplace to Tokyo. Secretly covets Lee Dynasty porcelain and a bedroom with a view of Everest

STRAITSKITCHEN

Enrica Fiorentini Delpani

Designer: Enrica Fiorentini Delpani.
Company: Studio Giardino, Brescia, Italy.
Projects: Small residential and commercial work including modernising traditional houses, new build villas, offices and shops.

Tirelessly passionate, she would like the whole world to understand Italian and enjoy life's simple pleasures. Fantasises about a bath filled with crème caramel. Wishes she took more care of herself. Thinks the electric light bulb worthy of worship and will give everyone she knows flowerpots planted with white tulip bulbs this Christmas

Orla Collins

Designer: Orla Collins.
Company: Purple Design, London.
Projects: Small practice providing a highly personalised service, mainly in the residential sector.

Big-mouthed Irish Catholic who wishes she could be free from guilt and learn to keep her opinions to herself. Perfection is a large glass of wine and Desperate Housewives, ideally watched from the comfort of George Clooney's chest. Thinks the world would be a better place without makeover shows. A wannabe bank robber, she dreams of racing cars around the Amalfi Coast and being more focused in her personal life

Angelos Angelopoulos

Designer: Angelos Angelopoulos.
Company: Angelos Angelopoulos, Athens, Greece.
Projects: Hotels in Greece, Cyprus, Istanbul and
New York, plus restaurants, showrooms and
private houses and apartments.

Alternative therapy addict with a serious Parthenon complex, he would like to have designed it and to be able to see it when he works, eats and sleeps

Categorically opposed to materialism and ambition, his greatest achievement so far is his relationship with himself and an award from Condé Nast Traveller

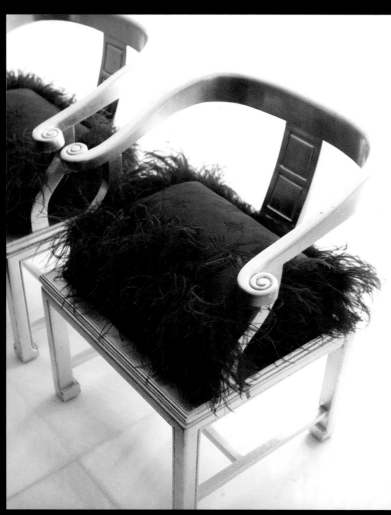

Has stayed in more sexy hotels than he can remember, gives love through his job and is still searching for his soul

Helene Forbes Hennie

Designer: Helene Forbes Hennie.
Company: Hennie Interiors, Oslo, Norway.
Projects: Small, focused design practice taking on high end residential projects plus offices, restaurants and hotels.

Would like to work for Armani and wishes she designed the Chrysler Building in New York but would not change a thing about her life

Giano Goncalves

Designer: Giano Goncalves.
Company: Ana d' Arfet, Funchal, Portugal.
Projects: Interior design shop plus architecture and interior decoration studio, taking on private houses plus hotels, golf clubhouses, restaurants, offices and nightclubs.

Precocious shop-keeper with a washboard stomach who wishes he was less shy. Would like to work on Ipanema Beach and dance all night long, as long as he had a good pillow and a comfortable bed waiting for him. Wishes he could talk to fish and throw a party in the Great Palace of Borgia

Zeynep Fadillioglu

Designer: Zeynep Fadillioglu.
Company: ZF Design, Istanbul, Turkey.
Projects: Private houses and commercial commissions including hotel, restaurant and exhibition design.

Richard Burton fan who valu
dictum 'live and let live'. Attem
learn how to cook, she could n
of her daughter. Curses the m

her personal space and lives by the

ng not to take life too seriously and to

ve without her corkscrew and the love

ent that the babyshower was invented

Dreams of an end to bird flu and a chance to take part on an archaeological dig

Rabih Hage

not a bird

Designer: Rabih Hage.
Company: Rabih Hage, London.
Projects: Interior designer and gallery owner who combines art pieces with his own furniture in residential and commercial projects. He is currently working on the design of the Design Club at Chelsea Harbour Design Centre.

Sweet-toothed dreamer in comfortable shoes who is still waiting to reach his full potential. Wishes he could keep to his diet and slim down a little and stop having to answer other people's telephone calls

Could not operate without his spectacles and a bottle opener but could do without disco fever. Loves the sound of Bora Bora and the word 'encore' is music to his ears. Would like to design a new version of the hanging gardens of Babylon

Susan White

Designer: Susan White.
Company: IGGI, Surrey.
Projects: Commercial and residential.

Vertically challenged arachnophobe with a disdain for bureaucracy and a desire to procreate. Has no greater achievement than getting married to her soul mate and finds nothing more complimentary than the words 'I love you'. Would dearly love a Mercedes SL Gullwing, the contents of the Louvre and a bit of work experience with Coco Chanel. Thinks shabby chic should be outlawed and dreams of playing Supermarket Sweep at Tiffany

Shoe fetishist and potential Minister for Culture, she would like to get closer to the England Rugby team, preferably in their changing room

Graham Green & Michael Keech

Designers: Graham Green & Michael Keech.
Company: Keech Green, London.
Projects: High end residential refurbishment.

Technophobic amateur pianist with lofty aspirations and a few pounds to shed. Would like to live at Cliveden, party at Chatsworth and spy on Buckingham Palace but takes most pleasure from the simple things in life: his dog, his partner, white sheets, sea views and a lot of cups of tea. Would happily destroy all speed bumps with a pick axe and smash every UPVC window in the country

Graham Green

Nini Andrade Silva

Designer: Nini Andrade Silva.
Company: Esboco Interiores, Funchal, Madeira.
Projects: Contemporary houses and restaurants
and international hotels for Enotel and Aquapura.
Currently designing a range of furniture.

Instinctive, enthusiastic potential pebble-worshipper with a God-given gift to create, she likes to see the sparkle in a client's eyes when a project is completed. Finds energy in wearing a turquoise ring and would like to own a large, perfect crystal

Big on Life's Adventures

Would like to stay on her isl
Found beauty under a goose d
romance on a circular bed in

d but open offices worldwide.
vn duvet in a Swiss chalet and
ne Portobello Hotel in London

Tony Stavish

Designer: Tony Stavish.
Company: A W Stavish Designs, Chicago,
Illinois, USA. Projects: A broad range of
high end residential projects from historic
renovation to new construction.

Loved by small children and animals, he has nightmares about wet suede and dry cleaning. Could not live without a commercial grade toaster for the ultimate snack but wishes he had longer lunches at work. Would like to erase all signs of ageing and eradicate the ranch-style house from the American consciousness. Would not mind falling asleep on the soft, furry underbelly of a lioness napping in the afternoon sun

Kunihide Oshinomi

Designer: Kunihide Oshinomi.
Company: K/O Design Studio, Tokyo, Japan.
Projects: Architectural, interior and product design in the retail, residential and leisure sector throughout Japan and Asia.

Self-confessed design addict with a hand in anything from a skyscraper to a door handle and an eye for a design utopia. Would gladly live in the Design Museum, model himself on Le Corbusier and eradicate the Post-Modern movement from history. Dreams of eloping to New York and building a Manhattan skyscraper, spending a week alone on Kona island and covering his workplace floor with marble

Alessandra Branca

Designer: Alessandra Branca.
Company: Branca, Chicago, USA.
Projects: Private residential and commercial, with projects all over the USA but primarily in Chicago. Commercial projects include the Presidential suite at the Peninsular Hotel in Beverley Hills and the lobby at the Mayfair in Chicago.

Caring, conscientious native Italian mother in danger of losing patience. Longs for more time in the day, for her children to be fulfilled and for her friendships to be more focussed. Dreads being separated from her vacuum cleaner, abhors plastic furniture and is against all prejudice

On a mission to reinstate people's faith in decorating and to spend more time at the gym

Katharine Pooley

Designer: Katharine Pooley.
Company: Katharine Pooley, London.
Projects: High end residential interiors including yachts, ski lodges and Scottish castles.

Mountain-climbing mummy's girl who hates to fly economy and dreams of piloting her own 747. Would like to change her hair, land a helicopter on Everest and see mountain peaks from her bedroom window

Has designs on the Mona Lisa and the Tower of London and believes she has what it takes to inspire a cult. Would like to ban mini-skirts (to spare the world her knees) and to give every dog a home

Gustavo Horta & Debora Stock

Designers: Gustavo Horta & Debora
Company: Horta Stock, Sao Paulo, E
Projects: Interior and architectural
both residential and commercial, th
work being contract projects and d
of large residential condominiums.

Magical realists who would like to invent a 9 day week so as to have more time off. Potential tree-huggers, they want to party on the beach and ban all nuclear weapons. Will give everyone they know a happiness certificate for Christmas this year and plan to continue conversing with their dogs. Would like to be remembered as good friends by their friends

Ryo Aoyagi & Katsuhiko Motosugi

Designers: Ryo Aoyagi & Katsuhiko Motosugi. Company: Kanko Kikaku Sekkeisha, Tokyo, Japan. Projects: Large scale architectural and interior design projects in the commercial sector, particularly hotel and resort complexes.

Creative marathon runners who would like a few less wrinkles and a more balanced existence. They dream of doing aerobics in the presence of royalty and directing for Disney and wish they had designed the Great Pyramid of King Khufu and worked for Leonardo da Vinci. Would like to converse with King Kong and destroy the atom bomb

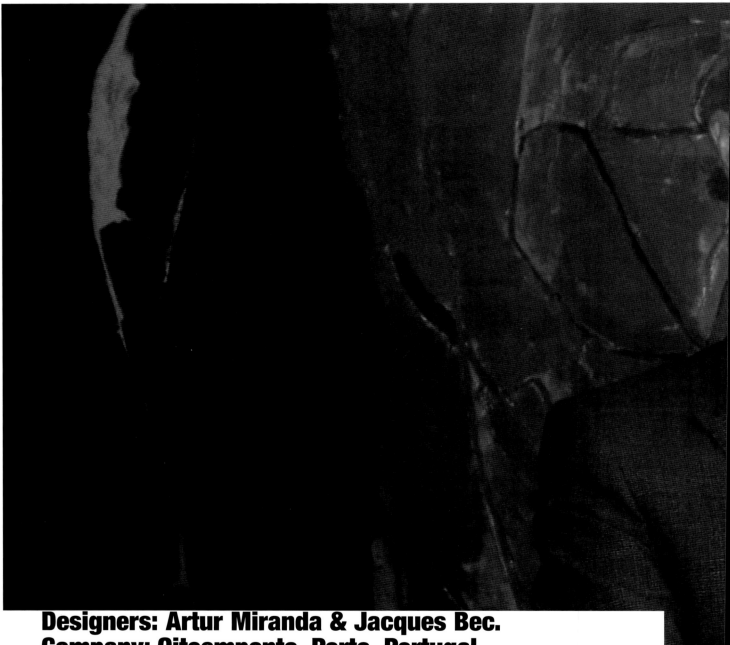

Artur Miranda & Jacques Bec

Proud and prolific caffeine addict
of set decorator and psychoanal
their own time machine and a ho
complain but do not go ne

**Designers: Artur Miranda & Jacques Bec.
Company: Oitoemponto, Porto, Portugal.
Projects: Predominantly private interiors, though
public and commercial spaces also taken on. Large
showroom in Porto housing a collection of furniture,
lighting and internationally sourced objects.**

they see themselves as a combination
t. Give them Venice without tourists,
e by John Lautner and they would not
them with an artificial flower

With a profound appreciation of extreme luxury and Madonna's shoulders, they fantasise about taking a suite at the Hotel Pierre in New York and playing xylophone for Pink Martini

Kathryn Ireland

**Designer: Kathryn M. Ireland.
Company: Kathryn M. Ireland, Santa Monica,
California. Projects: High end and homely, often
celebrity, residential commissions which are
both child and dog friendly.**

Unpretentious mother of three boys who longs to know what they get up to when she is not around. Life would be simplified with a private jet and a perpetual tan with no risk of skin damage

Wishes she had designed the Doge's Palace in Venice and could own a Barbara Hepworth sculpture. Would worship at the temple of the widget and stop global warming

Could not survive without her 4 over
of proportion. Wants to learn Spanis
homemade pasta at Giorgio's in Sant

ga. Abhors anything oversized or out
nd be mortgage free. Addicted to the
Monica

Laura Carter & F

Wannabe eco-warrior who would give ev
Christmas and longs to rid London of b
and spending more time on her beauty
Chanel and has been told she will look I
mother's engagement ring and her child

atrick Tyberghein

Designers: Laura Carter & Patrick Tyberghein.
Company: Carter Tyberghein, London. Projects: Architecturally led interior design company taking on residential, corporate, hotel and leisure commissions. Recent projects include a Golf chateau in Belgium, the interior of a helicopter and private houses in London and Dublin.

one she knows fair trade chocolates for
y buses. Dreams of talking to hamsters
ime. Would like to have worked for Coco
er when she turns forty. Treasures her
and in another life would be a barrister

Marc Hertrich & Nicolas Adnet

Designers: Marc Hertrich & Nicolas Adnet.
Company: Studio Marc Hertrich, Paris,
France. Projects: International commercial
commissions including hotels,
restaurants, company headquarters,
a retirement home and a nursery.

Impassioned archangel
of a magic wand. Influe
dreams of being taller.
nature (in particular

k-alike seeking permanent possession
d by Le Petit Prince of St-Exupéry but
gs to spend more time in contact with
cats) in a world without paperwork

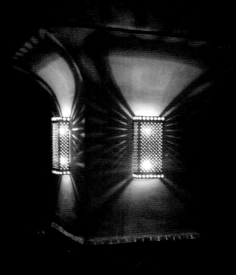

Would like to destroy the wind turbines of France and spend an invisible hour in the French President's office

Designers: Nick Candy & Christian Candy.
Company: Candy & Candy, London.
Projects: Luxury interior design and project management for the ultra affluent, from homes and yachts to private jets. Currently working on a new scheme on the site of Bowater House in Knightsbridge.

High-rolling, luxury loving brothers who are as passionate about design and property as they are about their yacht, Candyscape. As their workplace is perfection and their work is fulfilment, their only wishes are to have more hours in the day and to be free from the restrictions of technology

Widely travelled, they have their sights fixed on space

James Aman & Anne Carson

Designers: James Aman & Anne Carson.
Company: Aman & Carson, New York.
Projects: : High end private residential including Manhattan apartments, a Palm Beach home and a ranch in Santa Fe.

James is an art-loving, weight-watching, wannabe stand-up comedian who hates to be alone. Fortunately his peace-loving partner Anne likes nothing better than a hug. He would like to spend more time with his pug, Judy and less time in client meetings: she to surround herself with smiling people in cashmere and to grow a few inches taller. He would like a bedroom with maid service and a worldwide ban on shag pile carpets. She would rather be at the beach

Joseph Sy

Designer: Joseph Sy.
Company: Joseph Sy & Associates, Hong Kong.
Projects: Predominantly restaurant and hospitality design throughout Hong Kong, China and the Philippines.

Comic addict with an aversion to opulence. By night he swims breaststroke through the city skyline, by day he wishes to be more focused on work but he would not change anything about his life. Closet drummer, he would join Santana and he could not live without his hi-fi

Finds comfort in empty space. Would spend an hour invisible in a beauty pageant's dressing room. Would not elope without his wife

Shannon Martin

Designer: Shannon Martin.
Company: Shannon Martin Design,
Palm Desert, California.
Projects: High end Californian residential.

Optimistic chocoholic who sleeps on three pillows and dreams of falling from a great height, for whom the world would be a happier place without facelifts and automated answering systems

Would like to spend less time on useless worry and more on painting

Would like to switch places with Tina Turner but could not live without her heated hair rollers and her pit bull, Zero

Pia Schmid

Designer: Pia Schmid in collaboration with Christian Schwyter. Company: Pia M. Schmid Architektur and Designburo, Zurich, Switzerland. Projects: Architect working mainly in the hotel and restaurant sector, whose latest project is a cruise ship for the Nile.

Well-established, hard working motorcycle rider with a social conscience. Would like more sleep, less work and more focus on educational projects in the third world. Wishes she could speak more languages and live in a treehouse with a view of the desert

In another life would be a movie director. Loves Le Corbusier and Mies van der Rohe, loathes power and destruction. Happiness is sweet smelling herbs

Yoshiharu Shimura

Designer: Yoshiharu Shimura.
Company: Field Four Design Office, Tokyo, Japan.
Projects: Large scale commercial, including hospitals and cinemas.

Home town boy with royal aspirations for whom work is a pleasure. He longs for the power to deeply impress his friends and prays for mental and spiritual strength

Would like to have lived at the same time as Michelangelo and wishes we all spoke the same language. Would happily spend a week on another planet and control the seasons

Tanya Hudson

Designer: Tanya Hudson.
Company: Amok, London.
Projects: Residential, commercial and small architectural projects. Recently converted 2 beachfront houses into one home for Zoe Ball and Norman Cook and completed the modernisation of a 5 bedroom Edwardian family home in London.

Champagne drinking, heat seeking adventurer with a burning desire for a cleavage and her own Concorde. Likes nothing better than a low, firm bed and an on-tap masseuse, preferably in a luxury hotel in Bali - the Amankila would do. By night dreams of being a perpetual student with looming deadlines, by day on a mission to convince the world that she is the best thing since sliced bread

Joao Chichorro

Designer: Joao Chichorro.
Company: Soure & Chichorro, Lisbon, Portugal.
Projects: Private houses, hotels, shops and showrooms.

High living impatient plant lover who still doesn't think he has reached his full potential and finds the smaller things in life the hardest to handle. Would like to wake up with the body of Alexander the Great and the face of George Clooney in a world free of schedules, Art Nouveau furniture and price tags

Perfection is a good chauffeur and a permanent climate of 21 degrees. Happiness is his house in the country

Eddy Doumas & Lisa Kanning

A celebrity endorsed smoker and an ex-
aversion to stucco McMansions. Bot
tranquility of a private island in the A
35 for eternity, if only they could find

**Designers: Eddy Doumas & Lisa Kanning.
Company: Worth Interiors, Avon, Co. USA.
Projects: High end residential, often dealing
with second or holiday homes with an
emphasis on luxury living.**

cise shy champagne drinker with a combined
yearn to trade life in the States for the
ean Sea and both would like to stay fit and
healthy alternative to cigarettes and alcohol

He likes to be appreciated and wishes people were more honest, she longs

for prettier feet and a larger inheritance

She would rather be in Harrods, he has never had it better than in his cradle

Yukio Hashimoto

Designer: Yukio Hashimoto.
Company: Hashimoto Design Studio, Tokyo,
Japan. Projects: Commercial commissions
including hotels, shops and offices, plus a
range of lighting and furniture.

404

Light-footed, short-legged closet naturalist would like to end all suffering and travel to the moon. Relieved to be born a man and has no desire to change anything about his life. Would relocate his workplace to the Tokyo Tower while he spent a week on an Okinawa island sleeping on a futon and dreaming up ever more impressive designs

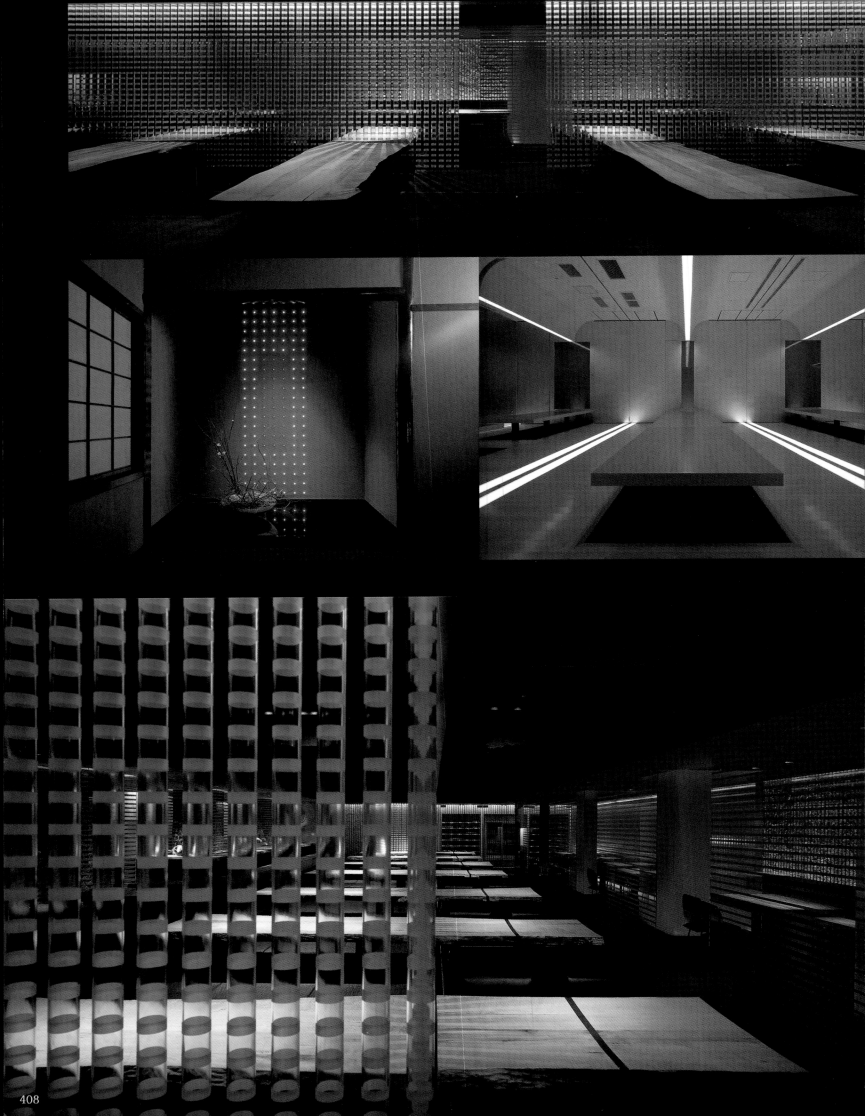

Brian Gluckstein

Designer: Brian Gluckstein.
Company: Gluckstein Design Planning, Toronto, Canada. Projects: Residential and corporate, extending to the design of custom furnishings and accessories. Recent work includes the Four Seasons Hotel Avenue Bar, Lobby and Tea Room, Toronto and the Mississauga Golf and Country Club.

Gun-hating book
worm with a
burning desire t
be Martha
Stewart. At a
push would go to
Lake Como or
Brazil but happi
in his own bed.
Wouldn't direct a
film, join a rock
band or change
single thing abo

Would be tempted to fall asleep on his partner and talk to horses. Might contemplate healing the sick but only on a very remote island and with no synthetic materials

Directory of Designers

4 Gail Taylor & Karen Howes
Taylor Howes Designs Ltd
29 Fernshaw Road, London, SW10 0TG
Tel 0207 349 9017
Fax 0207 349 9018
admin@thdesigns.co.uk
www.thdesigns.co.uk

12 Federica Palacios
Federica Palacios Design
3 Cour Saint-Pierre, CH-1204 Geneva
Tel 0041 22 310 22 76
Fax 0041 22 310 22 86
federicapia@yahoo.com
www.federicapalaciosdesign.com

20 Richard Adams
Richard Adams Interiors Ltd
36A Cheyne Court, Royal Hospital Road
London SW3 5TS
Tel 0207 352 1735
Fax 0207 349 2601
info@richardadamsinteriors.com

26 Jan des Bouvrie
Ontwerpstudio Jan des Bouvrie
Kooltjesbuurt 1, 1411 RZ Naarden
Postbus 5194 – 1410 AD Naarden
The Netherlands
Tel 0031 35 699 6219
Fax 0031 35 632 1574
info@hetarsenaal.nl
www.hetarsenaal.nl

34 Jaak Langenberg/Brigitte Vanzonhoven
Montagna Lunga
Torenstraat 3, 3530 Houthalen
Limburg, Belgium
Tel 0032 11 52 54 60
Fax 0032 11 60 14 64
montagna.lunga.bvba@pandora.be
www.montagnalunga.be

38 Cara Zolot & Elizabeth Kohn
ZK Interiors Ltd
1 Union Square West, Suite 511, New York,
New York, U.S.A.
Tel 001 212 924 6667
Fax 001 212 924 2380
info@zkinteriors.com
www.zkinteriors.com

42 Serdar Gulgun
Husrev Gerede
Caddesi Gozum, Apt. no 69 D. 3
80200 Tesvikiye, Istanbul, Turkey
Tel 0090 212 261 1840
Fax 0090 212 261 6084
serdargulgun@hotmail.com

48 Toshio Nagao
Kenmochi Design Associates
2-19-19 Shimo-Ochiai, Shinjuku-Ku
Tokyo 161-0033, Japan
Tel 00 81 3 3952 0195
Fax 00 81 3 3952 0197

54 Catherine Grenier
Atelier de Catherine, SL
Calle del Tato, 17, 28043 Madrid, Spain
Tel 0034 91 721 6150
Fax 0034 91 721 6151
cgrenier@atelierdecatherine.com

60 Silvio Rech & Lesley Carstens
Architecture & Interiors
32B Pallinghurst Road, Westcliff
Johannesburg, South Africa
Tel/Fax 0027 11 486 1525
Mobile 0027 82 900 9935
adventarch@mweb.co.za

66 Powell & Bonnell
236 Davenport Road
Toronto, Ontario, Canada M5R 1J6
Tel 001 416 964 6210
Fax 001 416 964 0406
preston@powellandbonnell.com
www.powellandbonnell.com

70 Colin Jennings
Douglas Wallace Architects & Designers
Fintex House, 19 Golden Sq, London W1F 9HD
Tel 0207 437 0882
Fax 0207 287 3583
tracy.oldland@douglaswallace.com
www.douglaswallace.com
Philip Treacy
1 Havelock Terrace, London SW8 4AS
Tel 0207 738 8080
Fax 0207 738 8545
www.philiptreacy.co.uk
Aurora Aleson
Tel +353 (01) 4534003
Gerry Barrett, Edward Holdings Ltd
00 353 91 865400
www.edwardholdings.com

78 Pip Isherwood & Karen Batchelor
Isherwood Interior Design Ltd
12 Imperial Square, Cheltenham
Gloucestershire, GL50 1QB
Tel 01242 226 966
Fax 01242 227 444
karen@isherwoodinteriordesign.com
contact@isherwoodinteriordesign.com

84 Sig Bergamin
Sig Bergamin Arquitetura Ltda
Rua Conego Eugenio Leite, 163 Jardim America
Sao Paulo, SP, Brazil CEP 05414 – 010
Tel 0055 11 3081 3433
Fax 0055 11 3064 3490
sigbergamin@sigbergamin.com.br
decoracao@sigbergamin.com.br

92 Christina Sullivan & Susan Bednar Long
Tocar, Inc
165 Madison Avenue
500, New York
NY 10016, U.S.A.
Tel 001 212 779 0037
Fax 001 212 779 0229
info@tocardesign.com
www.tocardesign.com

98 Philip Pelletier/Francesco Saporita
Vie Interieur Sarl Architecture
et Decoration D'Interieur
Rue des Bercles 3
2000 Neuchatel, Switzerland
Tel 0041 32 721 18 00
Fax 0041 32 724 41 43
concept@vieinterieur.ch

104 Helen Green
Helen Green Design Limited
6 Burnsall Street, London SW3 3ST
Tel 0207 352 3344
Fax 0207 352 5544
mail@helengreendesign.com
www.helengreendesign.com

108 Jestico + Whiles
1 Cobourg Street, London NW1 2HP
Tel 0207 380 0382
Fax 0207 380 0511
jw@jesticowhiles.com
www.jesticowhiles.com

116 Stefano Dorata
Stefano Dorata Architetto
00197 Roma, 23
Via Francesco Denza, Italy
Tel 00 39 06 808 4747
Fax 00 39 06 807 7695
studio@stefanodorata.com
www.stefanodorata.com

122 Allison Paladino
Allison Paladino, Inc
150 Worth Avenue # 219
Palm Beach
Fl 33480, U.S.A.
Tel 001 561 514 0155
Fax 001 561 514 0177
allison@apinteriors.com
and
445 Park Avenue S # 900 New York
NY 10022, U.S.A.
Tel 001 212 836 4042
Fax 001 212 836 4043

128 Luigi Esposito
Forma Designs
31 Cale Street, London, SW3 3QP
Tel/Fax 0207 581 2500
Mobile 07779 713 937
luigi.esposito@formadesigns.co.uk
www.formadesigns.co.uk

132 Luisa Reimao Pinto & Paula Gallego
K. arq-Arquitectos Associados
Rua Sousa Lopes
Lote 1759 Loja 1600-207 Lisboa, Portugal
Tel 00 351 917 23 3410
Fax 00 351 217 99 0691
k.arq@netcabo.pt

138 Tessa Kennedy
Tessa Kennedy Design Ltd
Studio 5, 2 Olaf Street, London W11 4BE
Tel 0207 221 4546
Fax 0207 229 2899
info@tessakennedydesign.com

146 Tim Harris
Tim Harris Interiors
PO Box 182, Mt Gravatt QLD 4122
Australia
Tel 0061 419 734 281
Fax 0061 734 222 717
timharrisinteriors@bigpond.com

152 Kiki M. Schröder & Peter Buchberger
KMS Interiors
Rauchstrasse 1, 81679, Munich, Germany
Tel 0049 89 901 094 94
Fax 0049 89 901 094 95
Mobile 0049 172 400 5996
info@kms-interiors.de
www.kms-interiors.de
www.rkpb.de

160 Christopher Dezille
Honky
The Loft Space
26a Oakmead Road
London SW12 9SL
Tel/Fax 0208 673 4188
Mobile 07786 131 186
dizzy@honkydesign.co.uk
www.honky.co.uk

166 Bernt Heiberg & William Cummings
Heiberg Cummings Design New York
9 West 19th Street #3 fl
New York, NY 10011
Tel 001 212 337 2030
Fax 001 212 337 2033
bheiberg@hcd3.com, wcummings@hcd3.com
mjacobsen@hcd3.com, contact@hcd3.com
www.hcd3.com
and
Heiberg Cummings Design Norway
Gimleveien 22, 0266 Oslo, Norway
Tel 0047 22 12 98 70
Fax 0047 22 12 98 79
eramm@hcd3.com
vkaasahoegh@hcd3.com

174 Monica Blinco-Lynch
Blinco Interior Design
PO Box 897, Hamilton, Q 4007
Australia
Tel 00 617 3216 1665
Fax 00 617 3216 1848
Mobile 0413 486 166
monica@monicablinco.com
www.monicablinco.com

180 Joao Maria
Abrindo Portas Dec, Lda
Praceta Jornal A Industria no 6 2900-362
Setubal/Portugal
Tel 00 351 265 547 660
Fax 00 351 265 547 661
Mobile 00351 91 253 6621
joaomariainteriors@gmail.com

186 Steve C. T. Leung
Steve Leung Designers Ltd
9th Floor, Block C
Sea View Estate
8 Watson Road
North Point, Hong Kong
Tel 00 852 2527 1600
Fax 00 852 2527 2071
sla@steveleung.com.hk
www.steveleung.com

194 Terence Disdale
Terence Disdale Design
31 The Green, Richmond
Surrey, TW9 1LX
Tel 0208 940 1452
Fax 0208 940 5964
terencedisdale@terencedisdale.co.uk
www.terencedisdale.co.uk

202 Mr Law Ling Kit & Ms Virginia Lung
One Plus Partnership Ltd
Unit 16A 332 Lockhart Road
Wanchai, Hong Kong
Tel 00 852 2591 9308
Fax 00 852 2591 9362
llk@onepluspartnership.com
admin@onepluspartnership.com

208 Susie Paynter & Teassa Paynter
Paynter Design
10 Walker Street, Christchurch
New Zealand Po Box 983
CHCH New Zealand.
Tel 00 64 3 3650 145 & 00 64 21 344 815
Fax 00 64 3 379 5265
tess@paynter.co.nz

216 Takashi Sugimoto
Super Potato Co. Ltd
3-34-17 Kamikitazawa
Setagaya-ku
Tokyo, Japan. 156-0057
Tel 00 81 3 3290 0195
Fax 00 81 3 3290 1650
intl@superpotato.jp

222 Enrica Fiorentini Delpani
Studio Giardino
Via Caselle 6
25100 Brescia
Italia
Tel 0039 030 353 2548
Fax 0039 030 353 2548
studiogiardino55@libero.it

228 Orla Collins
Purple Design
No. 1 Redcliffe Gardens
London SW10 9BG
Tel 0207 376 5414
Fax 0871 989 8817
info@purple-design.co.uk
www.purple-design.co.uk

232 Angelos Angelopoulos
5 Proairesiou st
116 36 Athens, Greece
Tel/Fax 00 210 756 7191
design@angelosangelopoulos.com
www.angelosangelopoulos.com

240 Helene Forbes Hennie
Hennie Interiors
Thomles gate 4
0270 Oslo
Norway
Tel 00 47 22 06 85 86
Fax 00 47 22 06 85 87
post@hinteriors.no

248 Giano Goncalves
Ana D'Arfet
Rua Tenente Coronal Sarmento
Edificio Costa Do Sol
No. 6 9000-020-Funchal, Portugal
Tel 00 351 291 757998
and 00 351 91 938 2356
Fax 00 351 291 744 396
anadarfet@hotmail.com

254 Zeynep Fadillioglu
ZF Design
A. Adnan Saygun Cad. Dag Apt. No: 72 D: 5
Ulus, Istanbul, Turkey
Tel 00 90 212 287 0936
Fax 00 90 212 287 0994
design@zfdesign.com
www.zfdesign.com

260 Rabih Hage
Rabih Hage Limited
69-71 Sloane Avenue, London, SW3 3DH
Tel 0207 823 8288
Fax 0207 823 8258
info@rabih-hage.com

266 Susan White
Iggi Ltd
The Old Parlour, Unit 6 Ockley Court Farm
Coles Lane, Ockley, Surrey RH5 5LS
Tel 01306 712 262
Fax 01306 712 073
Mobile 07970 356 791
s.white@iggi.co.uk

272 Graham Green & Michael Keech
Keech Green
414 The Chambers, Chelsea Harbour
Design Centre, London SW10 0XE
Tel 0207 351 5701
Fax 0207 351 5691
graham@keechgreen.com
michael@keechgreen.com
www.keechgreen.com

278 Nini Andrade Silva
Esboco Interiores
Rua Princesa D. Amelia No. 1
9000-019 Funchal, Madeira
Tel 00351 291 204370
Fax 00351 291 204379
esboco@esboco.com

284 Tony Stavish
A.W. Stavish Designs
2223 West Shakespeare Suite 1R
Chicago, Illinois 60647, U.S.A.
Tel 001 773 227 0117
Fax 001 773 227 9057
awstavish@sbcglobal.net

290 Kunihide Oshinomi
K/O Design Studio
2-28-10 # 105 Jingumae, Shibuya-ku
Tokyo 150-0001 Japan
Tel 00 81 3 5772 2391
Fax 00 81 3 5772 2419
oshinomi@kodesign.co.jp
www.kodesign.co.jp

296 Alessandra Branca
Branca Inc
1325 North State Parkway
Chicago, IL 60610, U.S.A.
Tel 001 312 787 6123
Fax 001 312 787 6125
abranca@branca.com
www.branca.com

302 Katharine Pooley
160 Walton Street, London SW3 2JL
Tel 0207 584 3223
Fax 0207 584 5226
enquiries@katharinepooley.com

308 Gustavo Horta & Debora Stock
Horta Stock Arquitetos e Associados
Rua Conego Eugenio Leite, 244, Pinheiros
Sao Paulo/SP, Cep: 05414-000 Brazil
Tel/Fax 0055 11 3082 5545
hortastock@terra.com.br

314 Ryo Aoyagi & Katsuhiko Motosugi
Kanko Kikaku Sekkeisha
No 17 Mori Bldg. 1-26-5 Toranomon
Minato-Ku, Tokyo, 105-0001, Japan
Tel 00 813 3 3507 0377
Fax 00 813 3 3507 0387

320 Artur Miranda & Jacques Bec
Oitoemponto
Rua de Tanger 1378
4150-721 Porto, Portugal
Tel 00 351 22 615 1724
Fax 00 351 22 615 1725
oitoemponto@oitoemponto.com
www.oitoemponto.com

326 Kathryn M. Ireland
Kathryn M. Ireland Inc
1619 Stanford Street
Santa Monica, CA 90404
Tel 001 310 315 4351
Fax 001 310 315 4353
kireland@kathrynireland.com
www.kathrynireland.com

332 Laura Carter & Patrick Tyberghein
Carter Tyberghein
Hyde Park House, Manfred Road
London SW15 2RS
Tel 0208 871 4800
Fax 0208 871 4900
info@cartertyberghein.com

338 Marc Hertrich & Nicolas Adnet
Studio Marc Hertrich
15 rue Gambey
75011 Paris, France
Tel 0033 1 431 400 00
Fax 0033 1 431 400 22
contact@marchertrich.com
www.marchertrich.com

344 Nick & Christian Candy
Candy & Candy Ltd
100 Brompton Road
Knightsbridge
London SW3 1ER
Tel 0207 594 4300
Fax 0207 594 4301
info@candyandcandy.com
www.candyandcandy.com

350 Anne Carson and James Aman
Aman & Carson Interiors
19 West 55th Street, Unit 3B
New York, NY 10019
Tel 001 212 247 7577
Fax 001 212 247 7977
info@amancarson.com
www.amancarson.com

356 Joseph Sy
Joseph Sy & Associates
17th Floor, Heng Shan Centre
145 Queen's Road East
Wan Chai, Hong Kong
Tel 00 852 2866 1333
Fax 00 852 2866 1222
design@jsahk.com
www.jsahk.com

364 Shannon Martin
Shannon Martin Design, Inc
73-200 El Paseo, Palm Desert
California, 92260, U.S.A.
Tel 001 760 341 9877
Fax 001 760 340 0698
shannonmdesign@msn.com

372 Pia M. Schmid
(in collaboration with Christian Schwyter)
Pia M. Schmid Architektur & Designburo
Augustinergasse 25
CH-8001 Zurich, Switzerland.
Tel 0041 44 221 08 48
Fax 0041 44 221 08 49
info@piaschmid.ch

378 Yoshiharu Shimura
Field Four Design Office
Fukoku Seimei Bldg.
27Flr 2-2-2 Uchi Saiwaicho
Chiyoda-Ku
Tokyo, 100-0011 Japan
Tel 00 81 3 3539 2881
Fax 00 81 3 3539 2883
shimura@field4.co.jp

386 Tanya Hudson
Amok
Unit 7 Town Mead Business Centre
William Morris Way, London SW6 2SZ
Tel 0207 731 6104
Fax 0207 731 6130
Mobile 07747 843 566
tanya@amok.co.uk
www.amok.co.uk

392 Joao Chichorro
Soure & Chichorro
Rua de Sao Bento no. 199, 7 Dto
1250-219 Lisboa, Portugal
Tel 00 351 21 395 1271
Fax 00 351 21 395 1268
soure.chichorro@clix.pt

398 Eddy Doumas and Lisa Kanning
Worth Interiors
PO Box 8369, Avon Co 81620
30 Benchmark Road, Suite 103
Avon Co 81620, U.S.A.
Tel 001 970 949 9794
Fax 001 970 949 4252
andrea@worthinteriors.com

404 Yukio Hashimoto
Hashimoto Yukio Design Studio Inc
4-2-5 Sendagaya, Shibuyaku
Tokyo, 151-0051, Japan
Tel 00 81 3 5474 1724
Fax 00 81 3 5474 4724
hydesign@din.ot.jp

410 Brian Gluckstein
Gluckstein Design Planning Inc
234 Davenport Road
Toronto, On. Canada M5R 1J6
Tel 001 416 928 2067
Fax 001 416 928 2114
longl@glucksteindesign.com
www.glucksteindesign.com